——— Stuff Every ———

GARDENER

——— Should Know ———

Library of Congress Cataloging in Publication Number: 2016946237

ISBN: 978-1-59474-956-8

Printed in China
Typeset in Goudy and Franklin Gothic

Production management by John J. McGurk

Quirk Books
215 Church Street
Philadelphia, PA 19106
quirkbooks.com

10 9 8 7 6 5 4 3 2 1

Stuff Every —

GARDENER

Should Know —

By Scott Meyer

QUIRK BOOKS

PHILADELPHIA

To Oma, who taught me that good food grows on trees and the rewards for hard work are sweet

INTRODUCTION 9

FOOD • How to Grow the Best Tomatoes Ever 12 • The Top 12 Culinary Herbs 17 • All about Berries 24 • Tree Fruit 101 28 • How to Grow Garlic 32 • How to Grow Spuds in a Bag 35 • 4 Perennial Vegetables 37 • Handmade Hydroponics 42 • How to Grow Belgian Endive Indoors 45 • Good Breeding 48 • **FLOWERS** • Tips for Hassle-Free Roses 52 • 10 Uncommon Bulbs 55 • Cut-Flower Favorites 59 • How to Add Color in the Shade 63 • 7 Flowering Shrubs to Try 65 • Meat-Eating Plants Are Real 69 • How to Force Flowers 74 • How to Divide Perennials 78 • **LANDSCAPE** • Edible Landscaping Basics 82 • Evening Garden Tips 84 • Finest Grass Techniques 86 • Small Trees for Any Yard 90 • Container Gardening Strategies 94 • 7 Ground Covers for Shade 97 • How to Prune Trees and Shrubs 101 • Mulch Always

103 • Native or Invasive? 106 • **PROBLEM SOLVING** • Weed Control Strategies 110 • 5 Homemade Pest Solutions 112 • Water Wisdom 115 • The Wonders of Compost 118 • How to Build Better Soil 121 • How to Extend the Growing Season 124 • How to Start Seeds Indoors 126 • How to Welcome Beneficial Insects 129 • Wildlife Control 131 • **RESOURCES** • Gardener's Glossary 136 • Seeds, Plants, and Supplies 139 • Essential Gardening Library 141 • Websites 143 **ACKNOWLEDGMENTS 144**

Introduction

I've been tending my own garden for 25 years, and each season I learn something new. Discovering different plants, trying tested techniques, facing unexpected challenges, and, yes, making fresh mistakes are my most satisfying yields as a gardener. You quickly realize that, no matter how experienced you are, there is so much more to know.

This book doesn't tell you *everything* about gardening—it couldn't, even if it were ten times longer. But it does put in your hands key insights and essential information about myriad problems, pitfalls, and triumphs. Some you may already know, but much will surely be new. See, most of us learn about gardening from experience and talking with others, rather than through comprehensive study, so our knowledge tends to have gaps. I'm hopeful that this book will fill in those holes, giving you a sturdier foundation in the art of growing plants and—best of all—inspiring you to grow as a gardener.

FOOD

How to Grow the Best Tomatoes Ever

The most popular garden crop is, has been, and probably always will be tomatoes. When you pick them fresh, they taste like summer—much better than the bland fruit found in grocery stores. Tomatoes are easy to grow, even in pots if space is limited. Here's how to raise the finest crop you've ever had.

- **Know the top varieties.** The tastiest tomatoes are the big beefsteak types that take all summer to ripen. The classic hybrids 'Burpee's Big Boy' and 'Park's Whopper' perform well in all kinds of conditions. Heirlooms, especially 'Brandywine' and 'Cherokee Purple', win a lot of taste tests, but keep in mind that these typically bear fewer fruits than the hybrids. If you love to make sauce or salsa, San Marzano and Amish Paste are meaty and flavorful.

Sun Gold cherry tomatoes start bearing just weeks after planting, and the super-sweet little yellow-orange fruit keeps coming well into fall. The vines of Tumbling Tom fit nicely in a hanging basket and spill over the sides.

- **Plant more than one variety.** Cold snaps, dry spells, hailstorms, pests, diseases, and other vagaries of the growing season affect each plant differently. Choose a few varieties to protect yourself from the horror of a tomato-less summer.

- **Buy smart.** Start with medium-size seedlings (rather than full-grown flowering plants) and look for plants with the sturdiest stems; they're likely to have vigorous roots. Pinch off any flowers before transplanting into the garden so the plant directs its energy into growing roots rather than forming fruit.

- **Choose the ideal location.** Plant tomatoes where they'll get 10 hours or more of direct sunlight every day during the height of the growing season. Drainage and air circulation are the best way to protect against fungal diseases, so be sure to space plants as directed in the growing instructions.

- **Prepare the soil.** Tomatoes need soil that's rich in organic matter. If your soil is dense clay, dig in compost to loosen it and allow roots to spread. If your soil is light and sandy, scratch in compost to help it hold moisture and nutrients for roots to feed on.

- **Plant deep.** When you bury the stems of tomato plants, they grow roots. The more stem you plant, the bigger the root system, the larger the plant, and the more tomatoes you'll harvest. Pull the sprouts and leaves off the stem up to the lowest full branch and bury the plant up to that branch. If you can't dig a hole deep enough, bend the stem to fit the hole. As the root system grows, it will balance the plant.

- **Train the vines.** Left untamed, tomato vines sprawl in all directions and expose your harvest to pests and diseases living in the soil. Metal cages hold them upright and are easy to arrange. Buy or make heavy-duty cages—

ideally from rebar—if you're raising beef-steaks so that the weight of the plant doesn't topple the cage in a storm. If you prefer more order, try bamboo stakes. Training tomato vines on stakes is most effective if you prune the plant so it has only one main stem, rather than several.

- **Feed the plants.** Tomato plants, especially young ones, benefit from a boost of nutrients such as those in liquid organic fertilizer made with fish waste and seaweed. It has a balance of nutrients, including calcium, a critical mineral for tomatoes. (Calcium deficiency leads to a common problem known as blossom end rot.) Water your tomato plants once a week with the fertilizer mixed in. Be sure to follow the packages dilution instructions—too much fertilizer can lead to big, leafy plants with little or no fruit.

- **Harvest at the right time.** You can tell when tomatoes begin to ripen: the deep green skin lightens just a bit. The hard part is waiting until they reach their peak. Even after turning fully red, orange, yellow, or purple, they may still be converting starches into sugars. Pick tomatoes that are firm but give slightly when pressed (the skin dents a bit from the pressure). If heavy rain is forecast, pick as many ripe fruits as possible before the moisture causes them to crack. At the end of the season, wrap green tomatoes in newspaper and store them in a cool, dry place. Check periodically; most will gradually ripen.

The Top 12 Culinary Herbs

Growing herbs is a simple, satisfying way to add homegrown flavor to your homemade meals. Here are the most popular ones for use in the kitchen.

BASIL (*Ocimum basilicum*)

The fragrant leaves on these 2-foot-tall plants have a lightly spicy flavor that's the foundation of pesto. A cold-sensitive annual, basil thrives in summer just about anywhere.

Best varieties: You'll find sweet Thai, Cuban, and lemon- or cinnamon-scented basils, as well as the more familiar Italian varieties such as 'Profuma di Genova'.

Tip: Start trimming off (and eating) the top leaves while basil is small to encourage branching, which will produce a bushier, more productive plant.

Chives (*Allium*)

These clumps of thin stalks come up every year, giving you green, oniony-flavored leaves all season long and pretty purple flowers. You can dig up a clump or chunk in fall, plant it in a small pot, and keep it in a sunny window to harvest as you need.

Best varieties: The most common variety of chives (*A. schoenoprasum*) has an onion-like taste, while Chinese or garlic chives (*A. tuberosum*) taste more like (no surprise!) garlic.

Tip: Chives are easy to dig up and divide every few years, so you can spread the plants throughout your borders or share them with friends.

Cilantro (*Coriandrum sativum*)

Cilantro leaves have a fresh citrusy flavor that's essential for homemade salsa. The dried seeds—known as coriander—are used to season chicken dishes, curries, and more.

Best varieties: When the weather gets hot, cilantro goes to seed and begins to taste bitter, a process known as bolting. 'Slo-Bolt' tolerates heat longer than other varieties.

Tip: If you want to use young cilantro leaves for garden-fresh salsa when tomatoes and peppers are ripe, plant some in midsummer.

Dill (*Anethum graveolens*)

The ferny leaves of this annual herb are ready to harvest from the middle of spring all the way into fall. The plants are easy to start from seed or to transplant.

Best varieties: 'Fernleaf' stays small, so it's ideal for growing in pots indoors or outside. For bigger, bushier plants, go with 'Mammoth' (aka 'Long Island Mammoth').

Tip: Grow dill in or around your vegetable beds because the small yellow flowers it bears in summer attract beneficial insects that prey on garden pests.

Mint (*Mentha*)

The mint family includes varieties with scents of apple, pineapple, and even chocolate. Nearly all are aggressively spreading perennials.

Best varieties: Peppermint has the most potent flavor; spearmint is milder. 'Mint Julep' has been bred for compatibility with its namesake drink.

Tip: Keep it in a pot, even if planting it in the ground.

Oregano (*Origanum*)

A shrubby low-growing plant with tiny flavorful leaves, oregano grows best in dry, sunny spots where soil fertility is low.

Best varieties: Many chefs prefer the flavor of Greek oregano to other varieties. Mexican oregano has a light citrus taste.

Tip: Oregano is notoriously difficult to start from seeds, but it's easy to grow from a transplant.

Parsley (*Petroselinum*)

Not just a garnish, parsley is a biennial but is typically grown as an annual.

Best varieties: Flat-leaf types, such as 'Giant Italian', have the strongest flavor; curly types, such as 'Extra Curled' or 'Green River', are milder.

Tip: Pick outside leaves so the center of the plant continues to develop new ones.

Rosemary (*Rosmarinus*)

In warm winter climates, rosemary grows year-round and can become a large shrub up to 6 feet tall. Elsewhere it is grown as an annual.

Best varieties: 'Blue Spires', 'Gorizia', and 'Tuscan Blue' lack the turpentine undertones of other varieties. 'Arp' is the hardiest.

Tip: Prune off a few stems weekly to encourage tender new leaves, which have the best flavor.

Sage (*Salvia officinalis*)

Sage is a perennial that can survive moderate winter temperatures, but cannot endure soggy roots.

Best varieties: 'Berggarten', is the most flavorful. The red flowers on 'Pineapple' attract humming-birds.

Tip: Plant sage where the soil drains quickly.

Sweet Marjoram (*Origanum majorana*)

Sweet marjoram has a mild floral aroma and flavor.

Best varieties: 'Golden-Tipped' is a pretty vari-ety with green leaves edged in bright yellow.

Tip: Add to food near the end of cooking—the heat makes the flavor much blander.

Tarragon
(*Artemisia dracunculus*)

This perennial has a sweet, delicate, licorice-like flavor that complements chicken, fish, and eggs.

Best varieties: French tarragon, which can be grown only from divisions or cuttings, is the most pungent.

Tip: Cut back brown foliage in spring, and divide the plant every third year to renew it.

Thyme (*Thymus*)

Thyme endures for years even in cold climates.

Best varieties: Lemon thyme has the best flavor and fragrance. Variegated varieties such as 'Aureus' or 'Silver Queen' are prettiest. 'Argenteus' is ideal for hanging baskets.

Tip: Thyme works well as edging for gardens.

All about Berries

Berries are probably the most rewarding crop you can grow—just pick and eat them right off the bushes. They require little or no maintenance, and aside from being as beloved by birds as they are by people, they're virtually problem free. Plant now and enjoy fruits for decades to come.

Strawberries

Strawberries bear baskets of sweet, juicy fruit from late spring into summer. The plants are annuals, but because they spread and generate new plants, you can keep a patch going for years.

Top varieties: June-bearing varieties produce their whole crop in a couple weeks, typically in June. They are the best option if you want all the fruit at once to make jam. Among June-bearers, 'Earliglow' starts yielding before most others do. 'Jewel' comes on a little later, a good choice where spring is long and cool. 'Honeoye' wins flavor comparisons. So-called day-neutral types bear only a few berries at a time, but the harvest goes on for up to six weeks. 'Tribute' and 'Tristar' are the most reliable in this category.

Key to success: Keep ripening berries off the soil with a layer of grass clippings or straw mulch to protect the fruit from mold and other fungi.

Raspberries

No garden crop takes less effort to grow than raspberries. With minimal initial investment, you'll be picking them for years. Buy one from your local nursery and plant it in full sun, giving it room to spread. Water when it's dry during the first summer. You might get a small harvest the first season, but in three years you'll be picking pints. After 10 years, you'll need pails to haul them in.

Top varieties: 'Heritage' is the most reliable red variety; 'Anne' is the most reliable yellow.

Key to success: In early spring, cut off the dried, brown canes that bore fruit last season. Also pull out new shoots where you don't want them. Raspberries will take over the garden if you let them.

Blueberries

With their beautiful white flowers in spring and brilliant red foliage in fall, blueberry bushes are often planted as ornamentals. But the purple-blue fruit in summer is the main attraction.

Top varieties: If you live where winters are cold, look for Northern Highbush varieties, such as 'Bluecrop'. In warmer climates, go with Southern Highbush varieties, such as 'Jubilee'. Blueberries are self-pollinating, but with most varieties you get a better crop when you plant at least two different cultivars.

Key to success: Cover bushes with netting to keep hungry birds from eating your crop.

Blackberries and Boysenberries

One thorny hedge equals unlimited tasty berries.

Top varieties: 'Shawnee' is the most productive blackberry. 'Apache' is thornless. Pick any boysenberry variety you can find.

Key to success: The canes spread aggressively but can be managed by diligent yearly pruning.

Currants and Gooseberries

These plants stay small and you need only cut out the dead canes periodically.

Top varieties: Choose from red, yellow, white, and black currant varieties. American gooseberry varieties bear smaller fruit than European types, but the plants are better adapted to the U.S.

Key to success: Currants and gooseberries grow best in partial shade and cool, moist soil.

Tree Fruit 101

If you have a sunny spot in your yard or even on a balcony, you can grow apples, peaches, cherries, citrus, and more. Dwarf and miniature trees reach less than 15 feet tall, yet bear bushels of full-size fruit. Many thrive in containers, so you don't even need a yard to get a good harvest.

Top Picks

Apples: Choose from countless varieties, including such favorites as 'Honey Crisp' and 'Golden Delicious'. In the tightest spaces, plant a columnar apple tree, which has stubby limbs that keep fruits close to the trunk.

Peaches: These come in early-, midseason-, and late-ripening varieties. Choose a later one where hard frosts continue well into spring; frost can kill the blossoms of earlier types.

Cherries: Pie (aka tart) types tend to be more

productive and less prone to problems than sweet cherries. Whichever you choose, cover the tree with netting to deter birds.

Citrus: Lemons, limes, and mandarin oranges don't tolerate freezing temperatures, but the dwarf trees grow well in pots that will need to be brought inside during winter. Meyer lemons and makrut limes are well adapted to containers.

Plant for Success

Ensure sunshine and fresh air. Give your fruit tree a spot that gets all-day sun and an unobstructed breeze and it will grow vigorously and problem free.

Mind the graft. Dwarf fruit trees are made by grafting a branch from the type of fruit that's desired to a rootstock of one that stays short. The graft line is visible as a swelling near the base of the trunk. Dig a hole, loosen the soil, and set the tree in the hole such that the graft line is 2 inches above the soil.

Stake well. A young tree's shallow roots leave it vulnerable to damage by heavy winds, so keep it secure and stable the first couple years.

Care Plan

Open the center. Air circulating through the tree prevents diseases and fungi. In late winter, prune off branches that cross into the center and block air flow.

Dare to disbud. You'll harvest the biggest and best fruit if you thin the crop each year. When fruit is the size of a jelly bean, choose one every 3 inches or so to keep on each branch and remove the others. Painful, yes, but you'll be glad you did.

Go organic. Pests and diseases can infest backyard fruit trees, but you'll keep your harvest pure by treating problems with safe and natural controls, such as horticultural oil and mineral sprays.

Potted Up

Go light. A 15-gallon container is big enough to grow a dwarf fruit tree but still light enough to move. Ceramic pots look nice, but plastic is more manageable. Fiber pots are best because they're lightweight and don't overheat (as plastic does), plus the roots are "air-pruned" so they don't encircle the pot and choke the tree.

Use super soil. Never use soil you've dug up outside—it holds too much water. Bagged mixes are fine, but try making your own. The ideal composition for a fruit tree is equal parts peat or coir (coconut husk fiber), mature compost, and vermiculite.

Provide food and drink. Give your tree a gallon of water every 7 to 10 days if it hasn't rained. Each spring and fall, scratch a couple inches of mature compost into the top layer of soil mix to nourish the tree and keep it bearing fruit for years.

How to Grow Garlic

Who needs more reasons to love garlic? It puts the zing in foods and protects us against all kinds of maladies, from common colds to vampires. More points in its favor: it's exceptionally easy and tremendously satisfying to grow. If you've only ever eaten garlic from the grocery store, you'll be amazed at how juicy and flavorful homegrown can be.

1. **Start in the fall.** Garlic needs time to chill, so planting is best done in fall before the first hard freeze. Small green shoots will emerge before winter. As soon as the weather warms in spring, thick green stalks with long pointed leaves will come up. Cover the soil with mulch (like grass clippings or straw) to keep weeds from competing for nutrients and water.

2. **Get bulbs.** You need just one or two garlic bulbs—the fresher the better. Supermarket

garlic is usually treated with anti-sprouting agents; instead, pick up heads at your local farmers market or garden center. You can also order them online.

3. **Plant cloves.** With your fingers, gently break up bulbs into cloves. Each clove will grow into a new bulb. Plant cloves in a garden bed of well-drained soil, spacing them about 6 inches apart. Plant the flat (root) end down and the pointy (shoot) end up. You can also plant cloves in large pots.

4. **De-scape.** Feed garlic every other week with liquid organic fertilizer made from fish waste and seaweed to ensure a steady boost of nutrients. As days lengthen, a long thin curlicue shoot may emerge. The shoot is the plant's flower, known as a scape. Cut it off and enjoy its light garlicky flavor sautéed with other vegetables.

5. **Harvest.** By midsummer, the leaves begin to yellow and then turn brown. Dig up bulbs when all the leaves have wilted, taking care not to hit them with the shovel. Brush soil off

bulbs and set them in an airy spot away from direct sunlight to dry out for a few days. Clip off remaining leaves and store the garlic in a cool, dry spot.

6. **Replant.** Set aside one or two of your best bulbs for next year's crop. Over time you will create your very own strain that's adapted to your specific conditions.

How to Grow Spuds in a Bag

If you have 3 square feet where the summer sun shines most of the day, then you can raise up to 15 pounds of fresh potatoes. No garden necessary! Here's how to grow potatoes in a bag (or a barrel—that works, too!).

1. **Get a fabric "grow bag."** These are available from nurseries or online, or just use a burlap sack. Fill it with a 50-50 mix of compost and peat or coir to a depth of about 4 inches. Dampen the mix, but don't soak it.

2. **Get some seed potatoes.** New potatoes grow from the eyes of old potatoes. You can buy seed potatoes, or if you have a few spuds sprouting in your pantry (you know you do), use those.

3. **Plant the potatoes.** Spread out about 8 seeds or sprouts on top of the soil mix in the bag. Cover them completely with more soil mix,

about 2 inches deep. Water well. Set the bag in the sun.

4. **Water when the mix gets dry.** In about two weeks, leafy green stalks will begin to sprout from the top of the soil. As they grow, add more soil mix up to the lower-most leaves. You'll see the tuber growing through the surface of the soil; shield it from the sun with more soil.

5. **Repeat.** Continue adding soil to the lower-most leaves and water when the mix is dry.

6. **Harvest.** In 6 to 8 weeks, the leaves begin to yellow and the stalks will brown. When they have all fallen over, it's time to harvest. Gently dump out the contents of the bag and root around for your buried treasure—the best-tasting potatoes you've ever had.

4 Perennial Vegetables

Most vegetables start as seeds or transplants in spring and are finished by frost. But with these four crops, you can plant once and reap the bounty every season for years to come. Even better, they become more productive as they mature.

Because perennial vegetables have extensive root systems that need to sustain the plants from season to season, you should grow them in dedicated beds that will be undisturbed by digging or tilling. Prepare the beds with generous additions of compost to create conditions that help the plants get established. Keep the soil well hydrated while the new plants are acclimating and spread a layer of mulch each year to block weeds and conserve moisture. Then all you need to do is gather the harvest.

Asparagus

Start: Asparagus plants are either male or female. Male plants yield more harvestable shoots because they don't invest energy in producing seeds. 'Jersey Knight' and 'Jersey Giant' are two widely adapted all-male varieties. 'Purple Passion' yields deep purple spears. The easiest way to start a crop is with crowns, a cluster of roots joined at the top. Asparagus grows best in full sun and moist, well-drained soil.

Harvest: A few spears may come up the first season, and a few more the next. Tempting as it is to eat them, leave those spears to grow tall and sprout ferny branches. The foliage allows the plants to photosynthesize and store energy for the future. In the third season, you can harvest spears that are thicker than a pencil. Leave the others to grow ferny tops. Each season after, continue the same practice of cutting the thickest spears and allowing the others to fern out. You'll enjoy a hefty harvest of tasty asparagus spears each spring for the next 20 years or more.

Horseradish

Start: The two widely available types of horse-radish—common horseradish, which has broad crinkled leaves; and Bohemian, which has narrower smooth leaves—are similar in flavor and growth habit. Horseradish thrives in full sun but tolerates light shade and fares well in any type of well-drained soil. Unless it contains a sushi chef, one horseradish plant is usually enough for a family. Grow from plants or root cuttings set out in spring or fall.

Harvest: You can enjoy your first horseradish harvest one year after planting. Carefully dig away the soil from around the main root, taking care to free up the side roots and removing them at the same time. Horseradish can be an aggressive spreader; to control it, remove the entire root, including its branches, when you harvest. Then replant only the roots for the number of plants you want to grow the next season. Don't till soil containing horseradish roots or place the roots in the compost pile—you risk spreading the plant all over the garden.

Jerusalem Artichokes

Start: Also known as sunchokes, these plants bear attractive sunflower-like blooms on 6- to 12-foot stems. The tasty part is the crisp sweet tuber, which can be eaten raw or cooked like potatoes. Plant tubers in full sun and well-drained soil. Choose between white- and red-skinned varieties.

Harvest: Where winters are frigid, start digging up the tubers in late fall, two weeks after your first hard freeze. In milder areas, wait until midwinter to harvest. You can keep harvesting through winter as long as the ground isn't frozen.

Rhubarb

Start: This crop is sometimes referred to as "pie plant," since the tangy stems are an ideal partner for strawberries in all kinds of baked goods, but they are also used in Asian cuisine as a soup vegetable. (Be aware: The leaves and roots are poisonous.) Plant in full sun and rich, well-drained soil. Varieties come in shades of red to pink to green. The deep ruby-red color is the most popular, but the green varieties are often more productive and tolerant of high temperatures.

Harvest: Wait 2 years for new plants to establish themselves before the first harvest. In spring, clip or twist off the stems at their base. When the newest stalks are short and thin, stop harvesting until the next spring.

Homemade Hydroponics

You don't have to invest in a lot of expensive, high-tech equipment to grow a healthy crop of salad greens indoors. All you need is a basic plastic storage bin with a lid, a few supplies, and a low-cost light fixture. With this setup, you can grow nine plants in a space as small as 3 by 3 feet.

Materials:

9 seedlings, such as lettuce or other salad greens
9 rockwool cubes*
Opaque 10-gallon plastic storage bin with a lid
Power drill with a 2-inch hole-saw attachment
9 net pots with 2-inch diameters*
Water-soluble organic hydroponic fertilizer*
Grow light or LED light fixture

*Available from retail and online hydroponic suppliers

1. Poke a hole in each of the rockwool cubes and gently plant the seedlings.

2. Drill 9 evenly spaced holes into the lid of the storage bin. Dump out the shavings and thoroughly rinse the bin.

3. Replace the lid and place a net pot in each hole, making sure they fit securely.

4. With the lid on and all the net pots in place, fill the bin with water so that about $1/2$ to 1 inch of the pots are immersed (about 9.5 gallons in a 10-gallon bin).

5. Remove the lid. Following the package's dilution instructions, add the fertilizer to the water in the bin and stir well. Replace the lid.

6. Set one seedling into each net cup.

7. Place the bin so that the plants' top leaves are 2 to 4 inches from the grow lights. In about a week, the leaves will start to grow, and the roots will begin to extend down into the nutrient solution. The roots grow longer as the fluid level drops.

8. In about 30 days, you will have big leafy plants and only about 10 percent of the original fluid will remain. Harvest your crop. You can pull out the whole plant and eat it or just snip off leaves as you need them.

9. When you're finished harvesting, thoroughly clean the bin and rinse it well before reusing for a new crop.

How to Grow Belgian Endive Indoors

This gourmet vegetable can cost as much as $4 a pound in grocery stores. But you're a gardener; with a little patience, you can grow your own crop. Indoors. During winter. With no special equipment. Seriously.

1. **Plant witloof chicory seeds.** Witloof chicory is a leafy green with a texture like curly kale and a slightly bitter taste. Plant it in spring after the last frost.

2. **Let it grow.** Chicory grows like any other salad green. You can harvest a few of the early tender leaves, but as the days grow longer, the leaves taste increasingly bitter. Leave the plants to grow through the summer and into fall. Be sure to water deeply during dry spells so the plant develops a long deep taproot.

3. **Dig it up.** After the first few autumn frosts, dig up the plants, taking care not to break off the taproots (which look like white carrots). Cut off the green tops to 1 to 2 inches long.

4. **Replant.** Fill large nursery pots with peat, coir, or coarse sand and moisten the medium well. Replant the chicory roots in the pots.

5. **Store it.** Put the pots in a cool (60°F to 65°F) dark spot, like a basement or closet, and keep the soil damp by sprinkling it once a week or so. Cover the pots with a bag to prevent light from reaching the roots. In about 3 to 5 weeks, tight-leaved pale-yellow to white cylindrical buds, known as chicons, will begin to sprout. Be sure to keep them in the dark, because light turns them green and makes them taste bitter.

6. **Clip chicons.** When the chicons are 4 to 5 inches long, clip them from the root and rinse them thoroughly.

7. **Enjoy.** You can eat the leaves in salad or fill them with hummus or soft cheese for a

healthy alternative to crackers. Or try using them whole by braising, steaming, or baking them au gratin.

8. **Repeat.** Keep the roots moist and in the dark and they'll continue producing chicons until you're ready to start the outdoor growing season again.

Good Breeding

The genetic history of a plant not only affects its performance and taste, but it also has an impact on the environment and the security of our food supply. The four terms below show up on seed packets and probably in your newsfeeds. Knowing what they mean will help you pick the varieties best suited for your garden and your philosophy.

Open Pollinated: When you save and replant seeds of an open-pollinated variety, the next year's plants will have same traits—color, size, and so on—as their parents.

Heirloom: Open-pollinated vegetable and fruit varieties that were commonly grown and shared among farmers and gardeners before the early 1900s are referred to as heirlooms. Many have unique attributes—for example, an uncommon color, in the case of purple carrots, or exceptional disease-tolerance, as with 'Brandywine' tomato.

Hybrid: Plant breeders work to improve varieties by giving them desirable qualities, such as a bigger yield or a more compact plant. By intentionally cross-pollinating varieties that have the traits they want, over a few generations they create hybrids that blend these attributes. Seeds marked F1 will produce plants with the traits described on the package, but plants grown from the seeds those plants produce will be different.

GMO: Rapidly expanding knowledge about genetics and new biotechnology tools have enabled scientists to transfer genes from one organism to another. In agriculture, that has led to the development of genetically modified crops, mostly corn, soybeans, and wheat. Many people are concerned about the impact on the environment and on human health and don't want to plant them. Although GMO vegetable varieties are available for home gardeners, they're easy to avoid by buying from sources that spurn them (see Resources, page 139).

FLOWERS

Tips for Hassle-Free Roses

The Queen of Flowers has a reputation as a fussy diva, but with a few simple steps you can grow stunning roses with surprisingly little effort.

- **Opt for shrubs.** Long-stemmed roses need perfect conditions to produce a few exceptional buds. Shrub roses are draped with beautiful blooms that last for weeks. Many rebloom in fall or periodically throughout summer. You can choose from dozens of varieties in a range of shades. Potted plants may cost more than bare-rooted ones, but establishing a growing shrub is easier than planting a dormant root.

- **Plant in fall or spring.** Late summer to early fall is ideal for planting roses, but you can also do so in spring. You'll see a few blooms the first season, and then in three to five years, the shrubs fill out and bloom abundantly.

- **Give them morning sun.** Fungal diseases, especially blackspot, are a rose grower's most common problem. One way to prevent them is to plant roses where they get direct sun, especially in the morning, so they can dry off the overnight dew that fungi breed in.

- **Manage drainage.** Soggy soil is another place that fungi grow, and it can also cause roots to rot. Plant rose bushes where rainwater drains away quickly. Mix compost into the planting bed to help manage moisture.

- **Allow breathing room**. Air circulation helps roses stay healthy. Leave at least 3 feet between rose bushes and any structures so air can circulate around them.

- **Water and feed.** In the first season, water newly planted rose bushes whenever the top few inches of soil dry out. Then you need only water during extended droughts. Ensure that roses have the necessary nutrients by scratching a granular organic fertilizer blended for roses into the soil around their base each spring.

- **Make your own quick cure.** Not only are chemical sprays and powders for treating rose-leaf diseases toxic, but they also don't work as well as this simple homemade formula: Mix a tablespoon of baking soda and a tablespoon of light vegetable oil in a gallon of water and pour into a spray bottle. Spritz affected leaves on an overcast morning. In a few days, the leaves will be free of mold and mildew and returning to their brilliant full green.

- **Prune and clean.** In late winter to early spring, clip off canes that have turned brown and brittle—they're done flowering. Also clip off branches (green or brown) that cross through the center of the plant instead of growing outward. Crisscrossing branches block airflow. Rake up the clipped canes and dead leaves, because rose pests colonize them before moving into the live plants.

- **Stop and smell!** Sure it's a cliché, but the fragrance of roses is one of the best reasons to grow them. It's a delight that can make even bad days better.

10 Uncommon Bulbs

When you think of flowering bulbs, you probably picture the usual spring bloomers—daffodils, tulips, crocuses, and hyacinths. Lilies and gladiolus may also come to mind. But the plant world offers a huge variety of bulbs that bring vivid colors and striking forms to your flower beds.

Alliums: These blooming members of the onion family open round flower clusters atop long stems. Most varieties are shades of purple, but some are pink, yellow, and white. The flower clusters may be as small as ping-pong balls or as big as softballs, depending on the variety. They come back year after year, and in sunny spots with fertile soil, they multiply like daffodils do.

Anemone: Even before the first daffodils poke through the soil, these so-called windflowers begin blooming on low-growing plants. They come in a wide variety of colors, from vivid to pastel, as well as different flower shapes. When the weather warms up, the flowers and their foliage fade away, leaving room in the garden for other options. Fall-blooming varieties are taller, reaching more than a foot high before flowering.

Arum: This family includes voodoo lily and orange candleflower. In late spring, the former sends up a chartreuse flower spike that's hooded like a Jack in the Pulpit. *Arum italicum*, aka orange candleflower, bears creamy white flowers in spring. Both produce stalks of bright orange berries as late summer turns to fall.

Camassia: Also known as wild hyacinth or quamash, camassia sends up spikes that are lined with blooms in pale yellow and baby blue (depending on the variety). The flowers open in late spring, after other bulbs are finished blooming and before summer perennials take the stage. In sunny but damp spots, camassia will multiply and spread. Bonus: deer do not eat these bulbs.

Chionodoxa: Glory of the snow is one of the earliest spring bulbs to bloom. It bears star-shaped clustered flowers with bright white centers atop dark stems with sparse, narrow foliage. It looks best planted en masse in sunny woodland borders and rock gardens, interplanted with other early spring ephemerals.

Eremurus: Foxtail lilies bloom in late spring with tall, graceful spires of dense flowers in shades of orange and yellow. The spikes open from the bottom up, rising above a ground-level rosette of long strappy leaves.

Fritillaria: In midspring, fritillaria reveals its bell-shaped flowers, which hang down from 1- to 2-foot tall stems. You'll find varieties in shades of purple, yellow, white, or green, some with patterns. Fritillaria are favorites of gardeners whose other bulbs have been plagued by deer or rodents.

Freesia: One of the most fragrant flowering bulbs, freesias are typically grown as cut flowers. They bloom about 12 weeks being planted them in spring (except where winters are mild, where you can plant them in fall). The trumpet-shaped upward-facing blossoms on nearly leafless stems come in different hues of yellow, blue, red, pink, and white.

Galanthus: Snowdrops open their drooping, milky-white blooms in earliest spring. They are very hardy, tolerating late frosts and even surprise snowfalls. Snowdrops look best planted in clusters or natural drifts.

Tuberose: A semitropical plant that thrives in sunny gardens in most climates, tuberose grows 3-foot high flower spikes with white 10-inch long blossoms. The slow growers can take weeks to appear, but their fragrance and unique flowers are well worth the wait.

Cut-Flower Favorites

Making fresh bouquets from blooms you grew yourself is one of gardening's most pleasurable rewards. These 10 beauties are the top varieties for cutting gardens because they bloom for weeks, have tall stems, and hold up well in the vase.

Cosmos (*Cosmos*)

Flowers: Red, pink, or white

Key to success: Help keep stems upright by enclosing them with twine tied to stakes.

Daisies (*Leucanthemum*)

Flowers: White petals around yellow centers

Key to success: Daisies are perennials, so plant them where you want them to stay.

Lace Flower (*Ammi*)

Flowers: Clusters of tiny white blossoms

Key to success: For long life in the vase, cut stems when a few flowers in the cluster are open, but most are still in the plump bud stage.

Globe Amaranth (*Gomphrena*)

Flowers: Lilac, pink, red, or white ball-shaped clusters

Key to success: Plant as close as 8 inches apart to encourage growth of long stems.

Love-in-a-Mist (*Nigella*)

Flowers: Frilly blue, purple, red, pink, or white petals in single or double rows

Key to success: Start these heat-sensitive flowers from seed in fall for early spring blooms.

Statice (*Limonium*)

Flowers: Pink, purple, or white funnel-shaped flowers open facing up atop stems that reach 5 feet tall

Key to success: For a vivid dried-flower arrangement, hang bunches in a cool, dry place for a few weeks, until petals are fully dehydrated.

Strawflower (*Bracteantha*)

Flowers: Multilayered petals in pink, purple, red, yellow, or white

Key to success: Start cutting when the first flowers open, and harvest often to encourage growth of new buds.

Sweet Peas (*Lathyrus*)

Flowers: Frilly blue, pink, purple, or white petals with a sweet fragrance

Key to success: Old-fashioned varieties work best where summers are cool and damp or winters are mild. If your springs are hot, opt for the newer heat-tolerant types.

Winged Everlasting (*Ammobium*)

Flowers: White petals form cups surrounding yellow centers

Key to success: Plant in soil that's low in fertility but drains well.

Zinnias (*Zinnia*)

Flowers: Orange, red, yellow, or white petals with yellow centers

Key to success: In muggy climates, opt for mildew-resistant varieties and plant them where air can circulate through.

How to Add Color in the Shade

Plants need sunlight, but many grow and bear brilliant flowers and foliage in the shadiest of places. If you want to brighten a dark spot plant a few of these dependable performers.

Annuals

These bloom profusely from spring to fall in the ground or in containers.

Baby blue-eyes (*Nemophila*)
Fuchsia
Impatiens
Lobelia
Tuberous begonia

Perennials

Every season, for years, these species bloom and proliferate.

Astilbe
Bleeding hearts (*Dicentra*)
Coral bells (*Heuchera*)
Hellebore
Primrose

Foliage

Colorful leaves are the main attraction of these plants.

Coleus
Hosta
Perilla
Sweet potato vine (*Ipomoea*)

7 Flowering Shrubs to Try

Woody plants are the backbone of beautiful landscapes, providing structure and connecting trees and flowers. Flowering shrubs do the job while offering big, colorful blossoms that attract birds, butterflies, and people.

Azalea

Why: They burst into bloom in the lull between spring bulbs and summer perennials.

Which: The 'Encore' series includes varieties that bear red, pink, or white flowers repeatedly from spring to fall.

Where: In the understory beneath tall trees or anywhere they'll get filtered sunlight. The soil should be acidic—like you find around oak and pine trees—and very well drained.

Hydrangea

Why: The big flowers last for months and can be dried to keep all winter.

Which: Bigleaf hydrangeas are best for mild climates. Where winters are frigid, plant sevenbark hydrangea (*H. arborescens*).

Where: Most varieties thrive in rich, moist soils and full morning sun with afternoon shade.

Lilac

Why: The scent is so intoxicating, you'll want to plant one near a window.

Which: 'Congo' is an heirloom variety that bears very fragrant wine-red flowers. Gardeners in the South can rely on 'Angel White'.

Where: Lilacs flower most abundantly in full sun. They can reach 22 feet tall and wide, so be sure to plant them with enough space for air to circulate.

Rhododendron

Why: It's one of the few evergreen shrubs that blooms, and in spectacular clusters of color.

Which: 'Orchid Lights' survives frigid winters. 'Ramapo' is a dwarf pink-flowering variety.

Where: Rhododendrons look natural in woodland settings and work singly in small landscapes.

Rose of Sharon

Why: Flowers open in late summer, when a lot is already done blooming.

Which: The 'Satin' series includes varieties that bloom in pink, violet, blue, or white.

Where: Rose of Sharon thrives in moist, well-draining soil. They can reach up to 10 feet tall, so give them room to expand.

Viburnum

Why: With fragrant white flowers in spring, dense summer foliage that turns brilliant colors in fall, and berries that birds flock to in winter, viburnums give you four seasons of interest.

Which: Pick from any of 150 different species.

Where: Viburnums grow in moist but well-drained soil in full sun to partial shade. Dwarf varieties may be less than 3 feet tall, but other types can grow as tall as 20 feet.

Weigela

Why: The dramatic display of big, colorful flowers starts in spring and lasts for weeks. Hummingbirds flock to the red and pink varieties.

Which: The blood-red flowers of hardy 'Red Prince' bloom repeatedly.

Where: Grow weigela in moist soil in full sun to partial shade.

Meat-Eating Plants Are Real

Carnivorous plants sound like an invention of science fiction, but they do grow in the wild and in gardens throughout North America. These four types of meat-eating plants all share a few basic attributes: they capture and kill their prey, they have a mechanism that allows them to digest it, and they are able to consume nutrients from it.

Boggy, acidic soils are typically low in the minerals vital for plants to survive. Nitrogen, the nutrient plants rely on for green growth, is in especially short supply. As a result, some of the plants that live in these conditions have evolved to capture and digest insects to turn their protein into nitrates.

Carnivorous plants don't track their prey; instead they have specialized leaves that act as traps. Some species lure prey with bright colors; others have extra nectar sources and guide hairs to snare unsuspecting insects. The protein-rich victim may be digested by the plant alone or in concert with partner organisms, such as bacteria. When the insect is dead, the plant absorbs its nutrients. Most carnivorous plants can grow without trapping and consuming prey, but they grow much faster and reproduce much better when they do.

Here are four you might encounter.

Venus Flytrap
(*Dionaea muscipula*)

The Venus flytrap, the best-known carnivorous plant, starred in the play and film *The Little Shop of Horrors*, but it is not really a man eater. It typically reaches only 8 to 12 inches tall and is native to the coastal plains of North and South Carolina, though it's also found in Florida, New Jersey, and other places with swampy conditions.

The Venus flytrap is an active trap: it moves as it captures its prey. Insects are attracted by a sweet-smelling nectar produced by glands on the inside of the trap. When the prey walks across a leaf, it touches trigger hairs that cause the trap to close. The plant then releases digestive enzymes similar to those in our stomachs, which break down and consume the insect's body.

American Pitcher Plant
(*Sarracenia* sp.)

Scientists have identified nine distinct species of American pitcher plant, nearly all of which are native to the Southeast coastal states, from Alabama to the Carolinas. One type (*Sarracenia purpurea* subsp. *purpurea*) can be found along the East Coast and into the upper Midwest and much of Canada.

American pitcher plants capture prey with passive pitfall traps. The traps are special leaves that form tubes with sweet nectar at the base to attract insects. The interior tube walls are either smooth or have hairs pointing downward that prevent insects from climbing out. As the tube fills with insects, digestive enzymes are released to break them down into nutrients.

Sundews
(*Drosera* sp.)

On every continent (except Antarctica), from tropical to temperate climates, you can find sundews growing in sunny but soggy conditions. The more than 190 species range from less than a half inch to more than 3 feet tall. Sundews are dainty plants, but they spell certain death for insects lured in by the sticky "dew" that appears to be fresh flower nectar.

Sundew leaves are lined with hairlike tentacles that have dewy drops on their tips. Insects that land are easily captured, much in the same way as in a spider's web. When an insect is caught, the tentacles wrap around it and hold it tight to prevent escape while the digestive juices go to work extracting nutrients.

Bladderworts
(*Utricularia* sp.)

The largest group of carnivorous plants, bladderworts include more than 200 species found around the world. Many grow in waterlogged soils such as bogs; others are fully aquatic and live in water. Unlike nearly every other kind of plant, bladderworts are rootless.

The traps are specialized leaves that have a "door" into the center of the plant that only opens inward. When an insect touches one of several trigger hairs outside the door, it opens and creates a vacuum that sucks in insect and water together. Digestion occurs within 15 minutes.

How to Force Flowers

When you can't wait for winter to end, try bringing a little spring into your life by forcing flowering bulbs or branches into bloom. You don't need any special equipment, and all the know-how is right here.

Bulbs

Tulips, daffodils (or other types of narcissus), and hyacinths are all easy to coax into early bloom indoors. The bulbs are abundant in garden centers and from mail-order suppliers in fall, which is the time to buy them.

1. **Prepare containers.** You need containers—terracotta, ceramic, or plastic pots or wooden boxes—with holes that allow water to run out. Cover the drainage holes with plastic screening to keep the soil from washing away.

Then fill the containers three-quarters with a blend of peat or coir, perlite, and bark.

2. **Plant bulbs.** Set tulip and daffodil bulbs with the pointy ends just poking out of the potting mix; add more potting mix between bulbs. For hyacinths and crocuses, cover with a thin layer of the mix. Keep the soil damp (but never soggy) throughout the process.

3. **Store properly.** Bulbs need a period of low temperatures—up to 12 weeks—to be stimulated into blooming. That's why we plant bulbs outside in fall for spring flowering. To force them to blossom inside, you need to mimic those conditions. You can store potted bulbs in an unheated garage, attic, shed, basement, or old refrigerator. The best location has consistent temperatures between 35°F and 48°F and stays dark.

4. **Bring them into the light.** After waiting roughly 12 weeks, it's time to bring the pots inside, but put them where they won't get direct light for the first couple weeks; begin watering them. Soon they'll be sprouting stalks

and leaves, followed by big colorful flowers, 4 to 6 weeks after being brought in from the cold. Next, just sit back and think spring!

Branches

As soon as daytime temperatures in late winter rise above freezing, you can gather branches from spring-flowering shrubs such as forsythia, dogwood, and lilac to trigger them to bloom inside your home.

1. **Collect.** Look for healthy, young branches with lots of flower buds (these are usually larger and plumper than leaf buds). Cut branches 6 to 18 inches long; longer branches stand up more easily in vases. Make the cuts about $1/4$ inch above a side bud or branch so that no stub is left behind.

2. **Arrange.** Once indoors, make another cut on a slant just above the first cut. Put the branches in a vase or other container that will hold them upright. Add warm water (110°F) no higher than 3 inches up the stems.

3. **Wait.** Place the container in a cool spot away from direct sunlight. Add more water to keep the level at its original height.

4. **Enjoy.** In a few days or weeks (depending on the species), the buds will burst into bloom. Then you can move the fragrant flowering branches to a spot where you can see and smell them all day long.

How to Divide Perennials

The best thing about many perennials is that they propagate themselves, growing bigger and blooming more abundantly year after year. But when an established perennial produces fewer flowers, or if the center of the plant begins to die back while the margins thrive, dividing is the best way to revive it. You can also divide healthy plants to share with a friend.

1. **Choose the right time.** As a rule of thumb, divide spring-blooming flowers in fall, and summer bloomers in early spring. The ideal time is just before a rainy spell, so that the moisture and cool temperatures help the plants recover from the stress.

2. **Prepare the plant.** If the ground is dry, soak the soil around the plant and wait 20 to 30 minutes for the water to drain. Trim back leaves and/or stems to 6 to 8 inches.

3. **Dig.** Starting at least 6 inches outside the clump, dig a circle around the plant. On a second round, push the shovel as deep as you can and begin to gently lever the plant out of the ground, leaving as much of the roots attached as possible.

4. **Divide.** Brush off excess soil clinging to the roots. With many species, you can easily break off clumps with your hands. To divide dense root balls, work the point of the shovel between stems at the center of the plant and push down firmly.

5. **Replant.** Replant divisions in the ground or in containers with potting mix as soon as possible. Set the plants at the same depth they were before you dug them up. Keep the divisions' roots consistently moist until you see new growth.

LANDSCAPE

Edible Landscaping Basics

Today, because of diminishing growing space, increased interest in food production, and liberated ideas about what's beautiful, many gardeners are integrating edible and ornamental plants to create landscapes that are both productive and visually appealing. Here are some tips.

- **Go colorful.** Plant hot peppers that turn red, orange, or yellow, 'Bright Lights' Swiss chard, or 'Bull's Blood' beets.

- **Think texture.** Add interesting foliage that complements flowers—like mesclun salad mix, bronze fennel, Tuscan kale or parsley.

- **Cover the ground.** Where you want low-growing ground covers, choose strawberries, thyme of any type, or creeping rosemary.

- **Choose flowers.** Flowering edibles such as chives, nasturtiums, and violets can brighten up both your salads and your borders.

- **Let vines climb.** Beautify unattractive structures like fences or railings by allowing vines and climbers such as grapes, scarlet runner beans, and summer squash to move on up.

- **Be fruity.** Blueberry shrubs not only bear sweet and juicy fruit, they also bloom with beautiful white flowers in spring, and their leaves turn a striking shade of red in fall. Apple and cherry trees put on dramatic floral displays before producing fruit. Dwarf varieties stay under 25 feet tall, making them easy to fit into even a tiny city yard or cramped suburban landscape.

- **Go organic.** You'll want to site edibles next to ornamental plants with similar needs for sun and soil. If you normally use pesticides and herbicides on the latter, avoid toxic chemicals if you're growing food.

Evening Garden Tips

If you work during the day, you're probably enjoying your yard mostly in the evening. Fortunately, you can have a landscape that's at its peak when the sun goes down.

Summer-blooming plants that put on a show in late afternoon and early evening include the aptly named four o'clocks, evening primrose, and moonflower. After dark, gardenia, nicotiana, and angel's trumpet perfume the air with heady fragrances aimed at luring in moths and pollinators.

Lighting

The night sky is one of the main reasons to be in your garden after dark, so keep lighting subtle and minimal. But safety comes first, so set up low lights along pathways to and from the house. They can be as sophisticated as a solar-powered light kit or as simple as votive candles inside jars. Either way, think of them as guides, not a runway. Less is more. You can buy all kinds of electric lights to create atmosphere around your seating area. For a fun DIY solution, float tea lights in a birdbath or water-filled container.

Pest Control

Mosquitoes and other biters get active around dusk. That might tempt you to buy electric bug zappers, but these noisy devices are ineffective against mosquitoes attracted not by light but by carbon dioxide (which you exhale with every breath). To keep populations under control, eliminate standing water wherever possible and set up bat boxes—bats eat mosquitoes by the thousands every night. Citronella candles also help keep pests at bay. For a plant-based remedy, try lemon balm, an easy-to-grow member of the mint family whose leaves are high in citronella. Crush a few and rub them on your skin for protection.

Finest Grass Techniques

A lawn is to your garden what a frame is to a painting. When it looks right, no one notices it. When it looks bad, it's all anyone sees. But you don't need a team of technicians or bags of chemicals to grow a thick and healthy swath of green. With simple techniques that encourage grass's natural habits, you'll have a lawn that's lush and trouble free.

- **Mow it high.** The most important step in healthy lawn care is also the easiest. Set the mower-blade level at its highest—ideally 3 inches. When grass is allowed to grow taller, roots penetrate deeper into the soil, where they gather more moisture and nutrients. Taller grass is also better able to compete with weeds than a scalped lawn.

- **Leave clippings.** Grass clippings are loaded with nitrogen, the nutrient that plants need for leafy green growth. Bagging or raking up clippings, then spreading high-nitrogen fertilizer, seems more than a little counterproductive (not to mention labor intensive). Instead, leave clippings on the lawn. As they decompose, they nourish the grass, earthworms, microbes, and other organisms in healthy soil that help grass thrive.

- **Seed, sod, or plug in fall.** The ideal time to plant or replenish a lawn is in autumn, when weather tends to be cool and rainy (or at least rainier than in summer). If you live in the northern half of the United States, cool-season grasses such as Kentucky bluegrass and turf-type tall fescue are best suited to your conditions. These grow from seeds, or you can purchase sod, which rolls out like a carpet. In the southern U.S. states, warm-season varieties such as zoysia and Bermuda grass fare well even through sweltering summers. They're planted as plugs, or root clusters with little leaves on top.

- **Feed in fall and spring.** All types of grass demand lots of nitrogen to stay green. The most important time to fertilize a lawn is in early fall, when it takes up nutrients before winter dormancy. Another feeding in spring, after grass has greened, is about all a lawn needs for the year if you leave clippings after mowing. Use slow-release organic fertilizers rather than artificial ones, which promote excessive and unsustainable growth.

- **Read the weeds.** The plants that sprout up in your lawn can be unsightly, but they're telling you something about the soil. Clover, for instance, is a legume that pulls nitrogen out of the air and "fixes" it in the soil. It grows where fertility is low. Broadleaf plantain, another common lawn weed, takes root where soil is compacted. If you understand what weeds indicate, you can find the right solution to keep them from coming back. Dandelions most frequently show up in soil that's acidic.

- **Spread corn gluten meal.** When weeds such as dandelions and crabgrass become more than a nuisance in your lawn, you may begin to consider toxic herbicides. Think twice—they pose a threat to the health of pets and wildlife. Instead, spread corn gluten meal, a by-product of corn processing that naturally suppresses the germination of weed seeds. It's available in garden centers and online.

- **Welcome moss.** No matter what claims the grass-seed packaging makes about how well adapted that variety is to shade, lawns tend to be sparse in low-light areas, a frustrating problem for homeowners. Simply put: grass is not the best ground cover under tall trees or in the shadow of buildings. Moss is much better adapted to these situations: it's green, tolerates foot traffic, and (bonus!) needs no mowing, weeding, or fertilizing. You can get it established with a chunk from a friend's garden or a "milkshake" starter kit.

Small Trees for Any Yard

The topic of trees tends to conjure up images of giant trunks towering 60 feet high. But most homeowners want specimens that will mature in their lifetimes and not dwarf their houses. The half dozen species described below are widely adapted to most of North America, provide shade for houses, and offer habitat for birds and other wildlife, all while peaking at modest heights of 30 feet or less.

Crape Myrtle
(*Lagerstroemia* sp.)

Fast growers that reach only about 25 feet tall, these colorful small trees bloom in midsummer to fall, when few others do. The flowers may be pink, red, purple, or white, depending on the variety; the bark is attractive, too.

Dogwood
(*Cornus* sp.)

The most common member of this genus, *Cornus florida*, grows to about 25 feet tall and wide at maturity, and its pink, red, or white flowers bloom in early to late spring. Unfortunately this appealing North American native is prone to insect and disease problems, so the similarly sized Japanese dogwood (*C. kousa*) may be a better choice. Its white star-shaped flowers open in spring, and leaves turn bright red in autumn.

Eastern Redbud
(*Cercis canadensis*)

Despite the name, these small trees thrive in the American Midwest states as well as along the eastern seaboard. They typically grow to about 20 feet tall in attractive vaselike shapes. They are some of the first trees to bloom in spring—their pink to reddish-purple flowers show up in March to May, before the leaves.

Flowering Crabapple
(*Malus* sp.)

The big, frilly pink flowers of flowering crabapples put on a dazzling show in early to midspring, depending on the climate. The tart little fruits, which typically ripen in August, are a delicious ingredient in homemade jellies and cider and a favorite food of suburban wildlife. Be sure to choose a dwarf variety, which grow only about 20 feet tall.

Japanese Maple
(*Acer palmatum*)

Stately maples are excellent shade trees that offer dramatic fall color, but they tower over any home. Japanese maples top out around 25 feet tall, and many of the 1,000-plus available varieties stop growing when they're less than 15 feet tall. Most have deep-red leaves from spring to fall, though you can find varieties with a more yellow-orange leaf color.

Witch Hazel
(*Hamamelis* sp.)

These flowering small trees reach only about 15 feet tall, but they won't escape notice. Their unusual spidery-looking flowers—which come in shades of red, yellow, and orange and are often fragrant—begin blooming in late winter, as soon as daytime temperatures climb above freezing. Choose from close to 100 varieties, all of which grow and bloom best in full sun.

Container Gardening Strategies

Pots make it possible to grow plants in small spaces or difficult climates. Here's how.

Explore the options. You can plant in just about any container, from basic buckets to hand-crafted pottery. Ceramic, terracotta, and stone pots look attractive, but they can be painfully heavy once filled with soil mix and plants. Plastic is much lighter, and good-looking options made of manufactured materials are readily available in nurseries and home-supply stores. You'll get the best of both worlds by hiding plain plastic pots within fancier heavy containers. The most important quality of any container is drainage, so be sure that whatever you use has holes in the bottom that allow excess water to run out. Plants sitting in water will drown (literally—roots need oxygen, which they can't get underwater).

Skip the stones. You may have heard that putting gravel, stones, packing peanuts, or other such materials in the bottom of containers is essential to good drainage. Though drainage is vitally important, adding anything besides soil mix reduces the space available for roots to spread and absorb moisture and nutrients. If the pot has a few small holes in the base, it will drain properly. If the holes are big and you want to prevent soil from leaching out, lay a couple paper coffee filters in the bottom before adding soil.

Mix the ideal soil. Soil from the ground is likely too dense (claylike) or too barren (sandy) for plants in containers. You can buy bagged potting soil, but pass on those containing blue or green crystals—potted plants don't need artificial fertilizers. Blending your own mix is better and less expensive. Mix equal parts peat or coir, perlite or vermiculite, and compost (homemade or bagged). This combination is loose enough for roots to spread, holds moisture and gradually disperses it as needed, and includes essential nutrients in exactly the form plants can use.

Use the right plant-to-pot ratio. When you put plants in containers, they tend to be small, so it's tempting to crowd them. A handy rule of thumb: a container should be about half the height of your plant at full size (or a third of the total height of the plant plus the container). So a 9-inch pot is ideal for an 18-inch-tall plant.

Water daily. Containers dry out quickly, so they need to be checked daily. Stick your index finger up to the second knuckle into the soil mix. If the mix isn't damp, the plants need water. Morning is the best time to irrigate containers, so that the plants can take up the water before it's evaporated by the sun and wind.

Feed weekly. Container plants need nutrients, even if your mix includes compost. Otherwise they may grow slowly and bloom sparsely. Fish- and seaweed-based plant foods are well-rounded fertilizers that come in concentrated liquids; just mix them with water and sprinkle them on. A dilute mix once a week is plenty (follow package instructions). Excess nutrients are to plants what overeating is to people: unhealthy.

7 Ground Covers for Shade

Grass doesn't grow well where sunlight is sparse, but don't leave shady areas barren unless you want them colonized by weeds. Plant one or more of these low-growing plants. They will obstruct weeds and help prevent erosion. Better still, many of them bloom, turning your darkest corners into carpets of color.

Carpet Bugleweed
(*Ajuga reptans*)

Height: 2 to 3 inches for foliage

This creeping evergreen perennial is exceptionally hardy and offers dense foliage that quickly fills in empty areas, smothers weeds, and inhibits erosion. The bluish to purple flowers appear in late spring, and the foliage turns stunning copper or purple tints in fall. It is exceptionally resilient, standing up to foot traffic once established.

Blue Star Creeper
(*Laurentia fluviatilis*)

Height: 2 inches

The little light-green leaves of this plant swiftly form a mat you can walk on. The small pale-blue, star-shaped flowers bloom from May through June. It is often used as an edging in front of taller perennials and in pathways between stepping stones.

Creeping Thyme
(*Thymus praecox*)

Height: About 3 inches, depending on type

Low-growing varieties of this evergreen herb gradually spread to cover bare spots. The prostrate types grow less than 3 inches high, whereas the mounding kind forms green or silver carpets that grow more than 5 inches high. Both bear pink or white flowers in spring and emit an earthy-sweet fragrance when walked on.

Ground Ivy
(*Glechoma hederacea*)

Height: 6 inches

Where you need a tough plant that can take almost anything but full sun, consider this aggressively growing evergreen creeper with its variegated leaves. It bears 5-inch spikes of tiny orchidlike flowers from March through July.

Sheet Moss
(*Hypnum sp.*)

Height: $1/2$ inch

For brilliant green color with a pillowy-soft texture, try this member of the genus *Hypnum*. It fares well even in poor, dense soil, so long as it's in the shade. It holds up to foot traffic and needs no maintenance once established. Look online for moss "milkshake" products, which make it easy to get it started.

Periwinkle
(*Vinca minor*)

Height: 4 inches

This hardy perennial is drought tolerant and holds up well to foot traffic. Its dark-green oval-shaped foliage is topped with flat-faced violet, pink, or white flowers from early spring through summer.

Sweet Woodruff
(*Galium odoratum*)

Height: 4 to 6 inches

The tiny green leaves form a dense mat that's topped with fragrant little white flowers in spring. Bonus: harvest the fragrant leaves for potpourri that's also a safe, natural moth deterrent.

How to Prune Trees and Shrubs

Woody plants need periodic trimming to stay healthy and look their best. For tall trees, hire an arborist. For those trees and shrubs you can reach with both feet on the ground, follow these guidelines.

- **Timing is everything:** Prune in late winter, so fresh wounds seal before growth begins.

- **Use the right tools:** Hand pruners cut branches up to $3/4$ inch in diameter. Lopping shears cut branches up to $1^1/2$ inches in diameter. For branches measuring 1 to 4 inches in diameter, use a pruning saw with razor teeth. You can reach higher branches with a pole saw.

- **Target your cuts:** Encourage air flow by removing branches that grow toward the center rather than away from the main trunk. Take out dead or dying branches, too.

- **Prune wisely:** Always prune just above a bud facing the outside of the plant, forcing the new branch to grow outward. For larger limbs, avoid leaving a vulnerable wound by making 3 or 4 cuts: About 18 inches from the trunk, cut one-third to halfway through the branch, on the underside. An inch farther out, make a second cut on the top of the branch until it breaks free. Before you sever the remaining limb from the trunk, identify the branch collar, which grows from the stem tissue around the base of the branch. Cut so that only branch tissue (wood on the branch side of the collar) is removed, but don't leave a stub, which may seal slowly.

- **Aftercare:** Woody plants naturally seal wounds. Prune no more than one-third of a plant's branches at a time. Wait until the following year if you need more cuts.

Mulch Always

A gardener's best labor saver is a layer of mulch. It blocks light from weeds and keeps soil from drying out, so you water less. Some mulches even pump up soil fertility as they decompose. So what's the right mulch for your garden? Depends on what you're growing.

Flowers

What: Grass, leaves, and straw are as effective in ornamental gardens as they are in veggie patches, but they're not very attractive. Shredded hardwood or pine bark chips, available in bulk and in bags, obstruct weeds and conserve moisture while giving your beds a more finished appearance.

How: Wood breaks down slowly, so spread a 3-inch-deep layer of mulch only at the start of each growing season. To feed the soil, start with a bottom layer of grass or leaves and top it with wood mulch.

Vegetables

What: Grass clippings, fallen leaves, and pine needles are ideal for mulching a food garden. They allow rainfall to percolate to plant roots while shielding the soil surface from direct sunlight. Even better, over time these soft materials break down into nutrients that plants absorb from the soil. Be sure grass clippings come from lawns not treated with chemicals—you don't want to poison your crops. Leaves work best when shredded—just run them over with a lawn mower that has a bagging attachment. If you don't have grass or leaves, use straw from a local farm.

How: Spread a 4-inch-deep layer on vegetable beds and continually replenish as the mulch breaks down. Cover the soil when you plant seedlings or after seeds have sprouted.

Trees and Shrubs

What: A barrier of hardwood or bark mulch protects trees and shrubs from lawn mowers and weed-eating string trimmers.

How: Spread a 3-inch-deep layer of mulch around trees and shrubs, but never mound it up around trunks. That invites disease and shelters bark-chewing rodents. Think of a bagel shape rather than a volcano.

Pathways

What: To block weeds in garden paths, roll out an old carpet. Then dress it up by topping with a few inches of pea gravel or shredded hardwood.

How: Wait to spread mulch until paths have dried out to avoid soggy soil for weeks afterward.

Native or Invasive?

Choosing plants for your landscape used to be simple: look at what's available from the local nursery and mail-order catalogs and check whether the plants you like need full sun, partial sun, or shade. Nowadays some plants are recommended because they are native, and others are discouraged because they're deemed invasive.

Native plants are indigenous to wherever your garden is. They will likely thrive with minimal care because they are well adapted to the conditions in your area; they also provide food and habitat for the wildlife that evolved with them. You'll see plants identified as natives in nurseries and online, but a plant may be native to the U.S. or even to your state, but not to your county. The North American Native Plant Society (nanps.org) maintains a database that specifies the region and type of landscape (such as woodland or prairie) where each species is natively found.

Invasive plants are, in many ways, the opposites of natives. They are species that were brought to an area intentionally or inadvertently and that then spread aggressively. Invasives are supplanting natives in many wild or uncultivated areas, overwhelming species that reproduce more slowly and reducing the food supply for small mammals, birds, and other creatures. Japanese barberry, for instance, was initially introduced as an ornamental shrub. It became popular with landscapers and homeowners for its deep-red leaves, adaptability to a wide range of conditions, resistance to deer browsing, and carefree maintenance. But the plant reproduces vigorously via seeds spread by birds and has quickly become a pest, crowding out many woodland plants. Yet nurseries still offer it. To avoid buying and planting an invasive species, check the USDA's Natural Resources Conservation Service database (plants.usda.gov).

PROBLEM
SOLVING

Weed Control Strategies

Nothing about gardening is guaranteed, but it's 100 percent certain that at some point you'll have to deal with weeds. Mulch (see page 103) is the best way to suppress unwanted plants, but when a few do break through, these tactics handle them effectively.

- **Get hands-on.** Pull weeds when they're young, before they have the chance to put down deep roots. Be sure to get the whole root. If soil is dry, moisten it first to loosen its grip. Repeat.

- **Hoe.** To clear weedy rows and beds, get a stirrup or hula hoe. The sharp blade pulls through the soil and cuts off weeds belowground.

- **Try corn-gluten meal.** A by-product of corn processing that's safe to eat, corn-gluten meal naturally stops seeds from sprouting. Spread it on garden beds in spring and it will control weeds through the season. Just bear in mind that any seeds you plant will also be affected, so use corn-gluten meal after your crops have sprouted.

- **Solarize.** Wiping out extensive weeds in a large area takes patience and a big sheet of clear plastic. Moisten the weedy area, then cover it with plastic (weighed down with stones or bricks). Sunlight heats up the ground through the plastic and, over the course of a growing season, will burn out the weeds.

- **Spray.** Citrus and clove oil sprays take care of sprouting weeds in pathways, patios, and other tight spots. Find these weed-control sprays online or at garden centers. Or buy the essential oil at a health-food store and mix a few drops in a quart of water. Coat weed leaves with the spray on a sunny day, and in a few hours the plants will have turned brown and shriveled. The next day, they'll be dead.

5 Homemade Pest Solutions

With a few items from your pantry, you can mix up your own safe, effective pest-control formulas. Before using them, test on a few leaves to be sure no harm will come to your plants. Also, avoid spraying in the middle of sunny days or you risk burning the plant.

Soap Spray

Works on: Soft-bodied pests such as aphids and thrips

Make it: Mix 1 tablespoon liquid dishwashing or hand soap (not containing bleach) and 1 tablespoon vegetable oil in 2 quarts water. Pour into spray bottle. Coat tops and bottoms of leaves.

Hot Pepper Spray

Works on: Chewing pests such as flea beetles and caterpillars

Make it: Puree $1/2$ cup chopped hot peppers (the hotter the better) with 2 cups water. Let sit overnight, strain, then mix in 1 tablespoon vegetable oil. Dilute with 1 quart water, pour into spray bottle, and coat leaves.

Baking Soda Spray

Works on: Blackspot and other types of fungal diseases

Make it: Stir 1 tablespoon baking soda, 1 or 2 drops liquid dishwashing soap, and 1 tablespoon vegetable oil into 2 quarts water. Spray on tops and bottoms of leaves.

Slug Trap

Works on: Slugs and snails

Make it: In the evening, place a shallow dish or plastic bowl containing a few inches of stale beer at ground level in your garden. In the morning, dump out the slugs and snails that were lured in and drowned.

Sticky Traps

Works on: Whiteflies, fungus gnats, and other little flying pests

Make it: Get yellow 3-by-5-inch index cards (or color white cards with a yellow marker) and glue them to popsicle sticks. Lightly coat both sides of the cards with petroleum jelly, then insert them into the soil near infested plants. Throw out the cards when they're covered with insects.

Water Wisdom

Fruit and vegetable crops need about 1 inch of water a week, 2 inches in especially scorching or dry climates. Plants may survive on less, but to grow and bear fruit, that's the minimum.

Hose-end sprayers, sprinklers, and watering cans handle the job, but they drench leaves. Leaves absorb very little water, and soggy foliage is vulnerable to fungal diseases. With drip irrigation—moisture delivered gradually to the roots—water isn't lost through surface runoff or evaporation, and soil can absorb the moisture and slowly disperse it. Here are the options.

Watering spikes: With empty 2-liter soda bottles and plastic attachments available through many gardening suppliers, you can make a DIY drip system. Just fill a bottle with water, thread on a spike, and push the spike a few inches into the soil. The fluid drains out in drops.

Price: Less than $10 for a set of 6

Soaker hose: Made with rubber that's been perforated, soaker hoses seep water along their entire length and saturate the ground about 6 inches in all directions. They're easy to install: just position the hose around plants, connect the open end to a standard garden hose, and turn on the spigot. Soaker hoses work best on flat surfaces and for short runs no longer than 100 feet.
Price: About $15 for 25 feet

Tape, tubing, and emitters: For the most direct watering of individual plants, set up a system that drips water onto the soil. Drip tape is plastic line with holes at regular intervals. It lies flat when empty and comes in rolls you can cut to your garden's dimensions. Tubing costs a bit more than tape but it's more durable and can handle higher water flow. You can also determine the location of the emitter valves based on a garden's layout. Use "elbows" and "tees" to lead branch lines up into raised bed. You can find tube kits scaled for container gardens, too. With either tape or tubing, you'll also need a pressure regulator, to avoid powerful household water flow from damaging the system, and a diverter to prevent dirty water

from flowing back into your home's plumbing.
Price: $40 to $120, depending on features

Timers: Attaching a timer to your irrigation system lets you water when it's ideal—in the early morning, so that moisture is absorbed before it evaporates. You can also go on vacation without asking a friend or neighbor to water your garden while you're gone.
Price: $20 for basic models

Deeply, Not Daily

Irrigating your garden frequently and lightly causes roots to cluster near the damp surface. Better to water once or twice a week, slowly so that moisture can percolate deep into the soil. Plant roots will grow bigger and longer, making for healthier and sturdier plants.

The Wonders of Compost

Compost is the answer to so many soil questions. How can you create the ideal conditions for any plant? Work compost into the bed. Your soil is heavy clay and holds too much water? Mix in compost. The soil is too sandy and doesn't hold water? Add compost. Fortunately for harried gardeners, nutrient-rich humus could not be easier to make. Here's how.

1. Find a spot that's about 3 by 3 feet and shielded from sight. If you like a neat look, you can buy or build a bin, but you don't need one.

2. Spread a layer of straw, fallen leaves, or shredded newspaper on the ground. On top of that, pile up grass clippings, dead plants, and other garden waste, fruit and vegetable scraps from your kitchen, and more leaves, straw, and newspaper. Add coffee grounds and eggshells, but no meat or fish scraps. If you have access

to bedding from barn animals, chickens, rabbits, or guinea pigs, toss that into the pile too. (Never put dog or cat waste into your compost. It carries harmful parasites.)

3. The ideal mix is three parts carbon (dry stuff like leaves and straw) to one part nitrogen (wet stuff like kitchen scraps and manure), but you can continue adding to the pile as you have the materials. If you have a lot of wet materials, try to alternate with more dry materials. A compost pile filled only with kitchen scraps can become smelly and attract pests, but it won't be a problem if you top each layer with dry material.

4. Moisten—but don't soak—the pile when it gets dry. When the pile is 3 feet tall, it begins to decompose. Stick a garden fork in it and you may see a puff of steam rise from the center, a sign that the process is working. Every week or so, move the broken-down contents at the center of the pile to the outside and drag the outside materials into the center.

5. If you turn the pile frequently and have the right balance of ingredients, your compost will be ready in about 8 weeks. Finished compost is moist and crumbly, with an earthy, sweet smell and no discernible ingredients. Spread a couple inches on your vegetable garden in spring, add a shovelful to every planting hole, and mix it with peat or coir for a perfect container mix.

Bins

A compost bin can help keep a pile of decomposing waste neatly contained and out of sight. Many municipalities give them away to residents to reduce the waste stream. Well-designed styles are available in nurseries or online. If you don't want to buy one, try building a bin with shipping pallets or simply encircle the pile with chicken wire. If yard space is lacking, look for a "tumbler" type, which can be set up on a patio or even a balcony.

How to Build Better Soil

The key to an abundant harvest is right below your feet. If you pay attention to building fertile soil, you'll need to do little else for your garden.

New Garden

Start with a test. A simple lab test will reveal vital information about your soil's nutrient content, pH level, and organic matter composition, and it's available for free or at a low cost from your state's land-grant university. The results will include suggestions for additives you can use to improve fertility.

Dig down or build up. Loose, crumbly soil allows roots to spread out. Use a garden fork or shovel to break up soil down to about 12 inches. If that's not possible, create raised beds by mounding soil at least 4 inches.

Pile on organic matter. Blend in organic matter after you loosen the soil. Compost is best because it has already begun to break down into nutrients. If you can't make your own, mix dried grass clippings, shredded leaves, and/or straw into the soil when you start the garden, and then keep a 1- to 2-inch layer on the surface.

Established Garden

Sow green manure. Legumes, such as alfalfa, and grains, such as buckwheat, are known as "green manure" because they add nutrients to the soil as they grow and after they decompose. Plant them between growing seasons to pump up your garden's fertility.

Skip the tilling. A powerful machine that breaks up tough ground is helpful when you're starting a garden, but repeated tilling damages soil structure, compacting it and inhibiting the flow of water. Mechanical tilling also kills worms and other small invertebrates that help decompose organic matter into nutrients.

Rotate crops. Many garden pests and diseases are specific to individual crops or families (such as squash or tomatoes) and can live in the soil from one season to the next. Changing up what and where you plant disrupts the problem cycle.

Container Garden

Choose a balanced blend. The soil you dig up in your yard is too dense for containers. Instead, use a potting-soil mix containing coir or peat, perlite or vermiculite (volcanic minerals that capture and disperse moisture), and compost.

Add worm poo. Worm castings are a concentrated source of nutrients that is ideal for container soil. You can buy them in bags or make your own with a worm bin, in which the crawlers feed on your kitchen scraps.

Ditch the chemicals. Synthetic fertilizers proclaim they are nontoxic to the environment, but they are high in salts, which accumulate and eventually leave the soil too acidic. Stick to organic fertilizers when feeding your crops.

How to Extend the Growing Season

By protecting plants from the cold, you can push the limits of your gardening season on both ends, early spring and late fall. Use these tools and tactics to insulate plants from killing frosts and plunging temperatures.

- **Cloches.** The French word for *bell*, a cloche was originally a large bell-shaped jar that 19th-century French gardeners placed over a plant in spring and fall to serve as a portable miniature greenhouse. Now you can buy cloches in all kinds of designs, or make cheap versions by cutting out the bottoms of plastic milk jugs.

- **Cold frame.** Inside a wooden box topped with a clear lid, plants can absorb sunlight while being shielded from harsh winds and frigid temperatures. Make your own from salvaged materials or buy one—some are set up to automatically open when temperatures inside get too warm.

- **Row covers.** With a light woven fabric that allows air and moisture to pass through, you can blanket large plants and whole rows in vegetable beds and protect them from frost.

- **Low tunnel.** Set up a knee-high frame, drape it with breathable plastic, and you have a small greenhouse environment where newly seeded crops and tiny transplants can get established safe from the cold.

Caution: Remember that the inside of these enclosures warms up toastily when the sun is high in the sky, even on cold days. Remove covers when air temperatures rise above 55°F to keep plants from overheating.

How to Start Seeds Indoors

You can buy seedlings of most garden plants, but starting your own from seeds indoors gives you many more varieties to choose from and lets you get your fingers dirty before the growing season begins. Plus, a packet of seeds costs about as much as a single plant or six-pack at the nursery.

You'll need:

Seeds of vegetables, herbs, and/or flowers (tomatoes, peppers, lettuce and other greens, basil, cucumbers, any kind of squash, and marigolds, zinnias, snapdragons, celosia, cosmos, sunflowers)

Soil-less seed-starting mixture, bagged or homemade (equal parts peat or coir, perlite, and finished compost)

Plastic seedling trays, peat pots, clean yogurt cups with holes punched in the bottom, or other small containers

Clear plastic lid or plastic wrap (transparent dry cleaning bags work well)

Fluorescent shop-light fixture

Small fan

Liquid organic fertilizer made with fish waste and seaweed

1. Moisten the soil-less mixture and fill each cell in the plastic tray with it.

2. Place 2 seeds in each cell. Check the seed package—some types need to be covered by soil, others germinate on the surface.

3. Cover the tray with the plastic lid or wrap.

4. Check daily to be sure the soil mixture stays damp. Gently mist it when dry.

5. Remove cover as soon as the first seeds sprout.

6. Set tray about 2 inches below the lights. Leave the lights for at least 14 hours and up to 24 hours a day. As the plants grow, raise the lights, but be sure they're never more than 3 inches from the tops of the plants.

7. Keep seedlings consistently damp but never soaking wet.

8. Place the fan so that a gentle breeze blows on the plants, helping them grow sturdy stems.

9. When the plants have their second set of leaves, begin watering them once a week with dilute liquid fertilizer (following package instructions).

10. If you started the seeds in a tray with small cells, transplant the seedlings to larger pots when they reach more than 4 inches tall.

11. About 4 to 6 weeks (depending on the plant) after starting the seeds, the plants are ready to acclimate to the outdoors, a process known as hardening off. For about 2 weeks, take them outside during the day and gradually increase their exposure to sunlight and fresh air.

12. Transplant seedlings to the garden on an overcast day. Be sure the soil stays damp for a few days so they can begin growing roots into the ground.

How to Welcome Beneficial Insects

Your most dependable allies in the battle against invaders are other insects. Ladybugs, lacewings, praying mantises, and many other species prey on those that damage garden plants. All you need do is make your garden hospitable to the beneficial bugs and they will discourage many of the destructive pests.

- **Plants:** Flowers with clusters of tiny blossoms appeal to the widest variety of beneficial insects. These include annuals such as sweet alyssum and baby's breath and perennials such as yarrow and hyssop. Let herbs, especially dill and cilantro, go to flower, and good bugs will flock to them. Intermingle flowers and herbs with your crops to attract the beneficials into your vegetable beds.

- **Water:** Good bugs need a steady supply of fluids. In the heat of summer, little puddles and other natural sources of water may dry up. Set a few shallow dishes of water around your edible garden, and the beneficials will come for a drink and stay for a meal.

- **Safety:** Pesticides can be indiscriminate, killing off beneficials as well as unwelcome pests. Abandon the toxic chemicals and allow the good bug population to grow to meet the supply of their food: pests.

Wildlife Control

Gardeners tend to love nature. But when deer, rabbits, groundhogs, and other critters munch plants and decimate gardens, the affection turns to frustration and even anger. Strategies like these can help minimize damage by deterring four-legged marauders.

Decoy crop. Animals comes to your garden in search of an easy meal. If you plant a few rows of basic, hardy crops like cabbage that are closer to the pests' habitat than your garden (say, near the tree line of a forest), the animals' appetites may be satiated before they reach your beds.

Scents. Stinky stuff like rotten eggs, garlic, hot peppers, and even scented deodorant soap can ward off pests with sensitive noses. You can buy or make sprays with sulfur and other strong-smelling ingredients to coat your plants. Hanging bars of fragrant soap in trees and bushes helps, too.

Light. Mammals that feed on gardens often come at night, and they're uncomfortable when they can be easily seen. Bright spotlights can be an effective deterrent—even better if the light is attached to a motion detector that switches on when animals sneak into your yard.

Water. A sprinkler attached to a motion detector gives unwanted animals a soaking when they pass by, sending them running for cover from the unexpected attack. You can buy devices like this online or set one up yourself. Either way, move it around your yard periodically so wily infiltrators don't learn to avoid it.

Noise. Loud or unpredictable sounds frighten off animals, too. Whirligigs and other noisy devices can work until the pests become accustomed to them. What works even better is a small radio set to an all-talk station, which can suggest that people are nearby. Just as with lights and water, a motion detector adds the element of surprise.

Fencing. When all else fails to keep four-legged munchers out of your beds, you'll need to set up a physical barrier. Electrified fences are most effective, but if that's not feasible, then try another kind. For deer, the fence should be at least 8 feet tall and slanted inward so they can't jump over it. If rabbits, groundhogs, or cats are the problem, the fence can be just 4 feet high but should descend at least 12 to 18 inches below ground to keep them from digging beneath it.

RESOURCES

Gardener's Glossary

Annual: Plant that completes its life cycle in a single year. Annuals sprout up from seeds, grow leaves and stems, flower or fruit, produce their own seeds, and then die. Though some annuals come back in the same spot year after year because their seeds drop on the soil and germinate the following season, the plants and their roots do not survive from one year to the next.

Biennial: Plant with a two-year life cycle. The first season it grows roots, stems, and a low cluster (or rosette) of leaves, which survive winter. The second season, biennials form flowers, fruit, and seeds. Hollyhock, foxglove, and sweet William are familiar biennials.

Biochar: Gradually heated decaying plant matter becomes charcoal, called biochar, that nurtures the beneficial microbes in the soil and increases plants' access to nutrients and moisture.

Bulb: An underground structure storing nutrients that ensures a plant's survival from one year to the next, even after the aboveground parts die back in winter. Daffodils grow from bulbs.

Coir: The fibrous husks from coconut shells that are ground and used as a light, moisture-retaining component of soil mixtures. A by-product of coconut processing, it can be a substitute for peat.

Corm: A swollen stem-base storage structure similar to a bulb. If you've grown gladiolus or crocus, you've planted corms.

Cultivar: A plant variety with distinct traits that have been cultivated by selective breeding, e.g. 'Brandywine' tomatoes or 'Knock Out' roses.

Habit: The shape a plant tends to grow into. Sprawling, upright, and weeping are different kinds of plant habits.

Hardening off: The process of gradually increasing seedlings' exposure to the sun and air before transplanting them to the garden. Ideally, this takes two weeks.

Humus: Dark, organic material that forms in soil when plant and animal matter decays; an essential source of nutrients for plants.

Hybrid: Varieties produced by controlled pollination to introduce desirable traits.

Mycorrhizae: A group of soil-dwelling fungi that have a mutually beneficial relationship with plants. Mycorrhizae thrive in humus.

Open pollinated: When pollen is transferred from male stamens to female flowers by insects, birds, wind, and/or other natural mechanisms. Seeds of open-pollinated varieties can be saved and replanted, and the next crop will have same traits as the first.

Perennial: A plant that grows back from its roots year after year. Daylilies, coneflowers, and phlox are popular perennials.

Variegated: Leaves or flowers that have multiple colors, in regular patterns or in streaks.

Vermiculite: A kind of silica used in soil mixes to hold and disperse moisture.

Seeds, Plants, and Supplies

Baker Creek Seeds
rareseeds.com

Burpee Seeds and Plants
burpee.com

Gardener's Supply
gardeners.com

Gardens Alive!
gardensalive.com

High Mowing Seeds
highmowingseeds.com

Johnny's Selected Seeds
johnnyseeds.com

Planet Natural
planetnatural.com

Raintree Nursery
raintreenursery.com

Renee's Garden
reneesgarden.com

Safer
saferbrand.com

Seed Savers Exchange
seedsavers.org

Seeds of Change
seedsofchange.com

Stark Brothers Nursery
starkbros.com

Territorial Seeds
territorialseed.com

Essential Gardening Library

The American Horticultural Society A–Z Encyclopedia of Garden Plants, Christopher Brickell

Armitage's Garden Perennials, Allan Armitage

Bringing Nature Home, Douglas W. Tallamy

Edible Landscaping, Rosalind Creasy

Four-Season Harvest, Eliot Coleman

How to Grow More Vegetables, Fruits, Nuts, Berries, Grains, and Other Crops Than You Ever Thought Possible on Less Land Than You Can Imagine, John Jeavons

Introduction to Permaculture, Bill Mollison

Four-Season Harvest, Eliot Coleman

The Living Landscape: Designing for Beauty and Biodiversity in the Home Garden, Rick Darke and Douglas W. Tallamy

Rodale's Ultimate Encyclopedia of Organic Gardening, Fern Marshall Bradley, Barbara W. Ellis, and Ellen Phillips

Second Nature: A Gardener's Education, Michael Pollan

Websites

American Horticultural Society
ahs.org

Dave's Garden
davesgarden.com/community

International Society of Arboriculture
isa-arbor.com

Land Grant Universities by State
nifa.usda.gov/partners-and-extension-map

Missouri Botanical Garden Plant Finder
missouribotanicalgarden.org/plantfinder/plant-findersearch.aspx

National Gardening Association
garden.org

The Old Farmer's Almanac
almanac.com

A Way to Garden
awaytogarden.com

Acknowledgments

I am deeply indebted to all of the gardeners who have shared their knowledge and insights with me. At the top of that list are my grandparents Hannah and Marcel Meyer, my in-laws Betty and Walter Smith, and my former colleagues at *Organic Gardening* magazine. I also need to acknowledge all of the dedicated master gardeners and researchers who make their findings available to the public.

Credit for the idea for this book goes to Tiffany Hill at Quirk Books, who guided the content and ensured the information was clear and thorough. My sincere appreciation to Catherine Strawn, the colleague who recommended me for this project.

Last but never least, I am grateful every day for the patience and loving kindness of my wife, Dawn. She has indulged my many gardening enthusiasms and never once questioned why I was digging up more of our lawn. From the garden in, she makes our house a home and fills it with the most precious yield of all, family love.